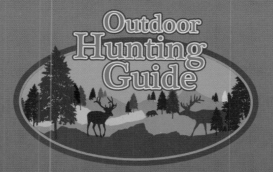

Outdoor
Hunting
Guide

Big Game

Connie-Lee McNeice

MEDIA ENHANCED BOOKS
AV²
BY WEIGL
ADDED VALUE • AUDIO VISUAL

www.av2books.com

AV² provides enriched content that supplements and complements this book
Weigl's AV² books strive to create inspired learning and engage young mind
in a total learning experience.

Your AV² Media Enhanced books come alive with...

Audio
Listen to sections of
the book read aloud.

Video
Watch informative
video clips.

Embedded Weblinks
Gain additional information
for research.

Try This!
Complete activities and
hands-on experiments.

Key Words
Study vocabulary, and
complete a matching
word activity.

Quizzes
Test your knowledge.

Slide Show
View images and
captions, and prepare
a presentation.

... and much, much more!

Go to www.av2books.com,
and enter this book's
unique code.

BOOK CODE

C240905

AV² by Weigl brings you media
enhanced books that support
active learning.

Published by AV² by Weigl
350 5th Avenue, 59th Floor
New York, NY 10118
Website: www.weigl.com   www.av2books.com

Library of Congress Cataloging-in-Publication Data

McNeice, Connie-Lee.
 Big game / Connie-Lee McNeice.
     p. cm.
 Includes bibliographical references and index.
 ISBN 978-1-61913-502-4 (hard cover : alk. paper) — ISBN 978-1-61913-506-2 (soft cover : alk. paper) — ISBN 978-1-61913-697-7 (ebook)
 1. Big game hunting—Juvenile literature. I. Title.
 SK35.5.M36 2013
 799.2'6—dc23
                          2012005575

Printed in the United States of America in North Mankato, Minnesota
2 3 4 5 6 7 8 9 16 15 14 13 12

122012
WEP031212

Project Coordinator: Aaron Carr
Art Director: Terry Paulhus

Every reasonable effort has been made to trace ownership and to obtain permission to reprint copyright material. The publishers would be pleased to
have any errors or omissions brought to their attention so that they may be corrected in subsequent printings.

Weigl acknowledges Getty Images as its primary image supplier for this title. Page 11, bighorn sheep droppings, courtesy of Kathryn Colestock-Burke.

Outdoor Hunting Guide

Big Game

Contents

What Is Big Game Hunting?

Hunting is pursuing an animal for food or for sport. In North America, many types of big-game animals are hunted. They include large **mammals**, such as deer, moose, and bears.

People hunt for many reasons. Hunters can use an animal's meat for food. They can use its furs for warmth. In addition, many hunters enjoy being outdoors. Big-game animals live in forests, near lakes, and in other natural settings. Going on a hunt can be good exercise. Hunters may walk for miles (kilometers) to find an animal.

People of all ages take part in hunting. For some, going hunting is a family tradition. Adults may teach children to hunt. Hunting can be done with a partner, in a group, or alone as an adult.

It takes knowledge and skill to track and pursue an animal. Hunters must learn about the animal and the places where it searches for food. They get to know the animal's **habitat**. Hunters must also know how to use hunting tools. They use bows and arrows or guns to shoot animals. Hunters must have proper training to use this equipment.

In 2011, the United States issued almost 15 million hunting licenses.

Hunting seasons vary in length depending on the **species** of animal and its location.

Theodore Roosevelt, who later became president of the United States, founded the Boone and Crockett Club in 1887. The hunting club has been keeping big-game **trophy** records since 1902.

Focus on Big Game

Deer, bighorn sheep, elk, moose, and bears are some of the most popular big-game animals in North America. The hunting season for most big game is in the fall. This makes it possible for the animals to raise their young earlier in the year. During hunting season, many hunters try to set records. They try to capture the largest animals.

Deer can be found feeding alone or in small groups at dawn and dusk. They like meadows close to forest edges. From there, they can make a quick escape into the woods. Elk **graze** in mountain meadows during the summer and in lower valleys in winter. Elk are often found in herds, while moose usually graze alone. They eat mainly water plants, tall grasses, and shrubs. Moose are great swimmers and will even go underwater to get their favorite food.

The mule deer is named for its ears, which look like the ears of a mule.

Bighorn sheep live high in the mountains. Each year, their horns grow larger. The horns of female sheep are smaller and shorter than those of male sheep.

Black bears are the most common type of bear found in North America. They live in many different habitats. Black bears are usually found in forests, but they also live in mountains. They travel large distances in search of food. Bears tend to live alone. Black bears **hibernate** through the winter months.

Big Game Animals

Bighorn Sheep

Bighorn sheep graze in the mountains. They live in the Rocky Mountains and are also found in Nevada, California, Texas, and Mexico.

Deer

Common deer include the white-tailed, black-tailed, mule, and Sitka deer. They live in North American forests and grasslands.

Elk

Elk prefer open woodlands. Sometimes, they live in swamps with pine trees. The largest numbers of elk roam the western United States.

Bear

Bears prefer forested areas with plenty of vegetation. Their diet consists mostly of grasses, roots, berries, and insects. They live throughout most of North America, from Mexico to Alaska.

Moose

Moose live in forests with lakes, ponds, streams, and swamps. They like areas where snow falls in winter. They live throughout Alaska, Canada, and in the northern United States as far south as Colorado.

In the plains of North America, early people hunted large animals called mammoths.

History

In the past, hunting for food was something people had to do to survive. Hunting big game was dangerous. Early people did not have weapons that allowed them to hunt from a distance. Using stone hand tools and heavy spears, they attacked their prey at close range. Hunters were often injured in the process.

Successful hunting required knowledge and strength. Sometimes, hunters chased a wounded animal for hours or days until it was weak enough to catch. Only hunters with good tracking skills could follow the animal's trail. Over time, hunters developed lighter and more effective tools. They shaped rocks by flaking off pieces to create sharp points. Then, they attached the pointed rock to a spear. The spear could be thrown only a short distance. A wooden throwing stick, called an atlatl, extended the spear's **range**.

Early people also developed the bow and arrow. The bow was light and easy to carry, especially when compared with the spear. The arrows traveled very fast over long distances.

In the past, Native Peoples across the plains of North America hunted bison. They used every part of the animal. They ate the best meat right away and made the rest into **pemmican**. Native Peoples used **sinews** for sewing and making bows. They made bones into tools and used the **hides** for clothing, bedding, and tepees. When people started to grow crops, hunting became less necessary. It became a sport as well as a way to provide meat.

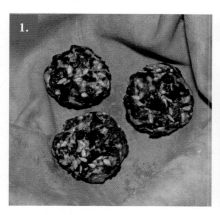

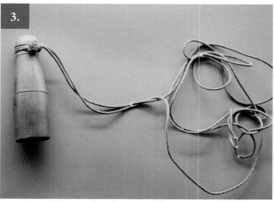

1. Pemmican cakes were often made from deer meat, berries, and seeds.
2. Native Peoples in North America first obtained horses for hunting from Spanish settlers.
3. Deer calls from the early 1900s used deer-like sounds to attract animals.

TIMELINE

2 million to 1 million years ago Early people in Africa had to get close to their prey to attack.

500,000 years ago Hunters in Europe began to use finely crafted spears when hunting.

64,000 years ago Bows and arrows were used in Africa.

15,500–13,300 years ago Large spear points were used to hunt big game in North America.

450 years ago Native Peoples on the Great Plains started riding horses to hunt.

Almost 400 years ago North American settlers used guns to hunt big game.

More than 100 years ago Hunting big game in Africa became a popular sport for Europeans and Americans.

Tracking

The more hunters know about the animal they are pursuing, the more likely they are to have a successful hunt. Using binoculars and a **spotting scope** can help hunters find game from a distance. Once hunters know where to start looking for an animal, they can begin a closer search. Animal signs include such things as game trails, tracks, droppings, beds, and marks made from rubbing on trees.

Game trails are small paths used by animals as they move in search of food and shelter. Tracks on sandy, muddy, or snowy trails often help hunters identify which animals are using the trail. Some hunters can also tell how long ago the animals made the paw prints. If the tracks are old, they may be partly filled with leaves, needles, or snow. Fresh tracks have sharper edges. Animal droppings also help hunters. By showing what an animal has eaten, droppings can tell hunters what kind of animal it is.

Binoculars are also called field glasses.

Animal Tracks

Animal tracks are the imprints an animal leaves on the ground or in snow. An animal can be identified by its tracks. Tracks can also indicate the direction an animal is traveling. They even show whether the animal was walking or running. Sometimes, tracks are not very clear. In these cases, other clues, such as droppings, can help identify an animal.

Deer

Tracks Droppings

Elk

Tracks Droppings

Bighorn Sheep

Tracks Droppings

Black Bear

Tracks Droppings

Moose

Tracks Droppings

Equipment and Clothing

Hunters can choose many pieces of equipment to bring with them. Some types of equipment are very important. These include a rifle or bow and arrow, binoculars or a spotting scope, and a good knife. The clothing that hunters choose is also important. Camouflage clothing is especially popular. This clothing has colors and patterns that help hunters blend into their surroundings. There are camouflage gloves, hats, jackets, and pants.

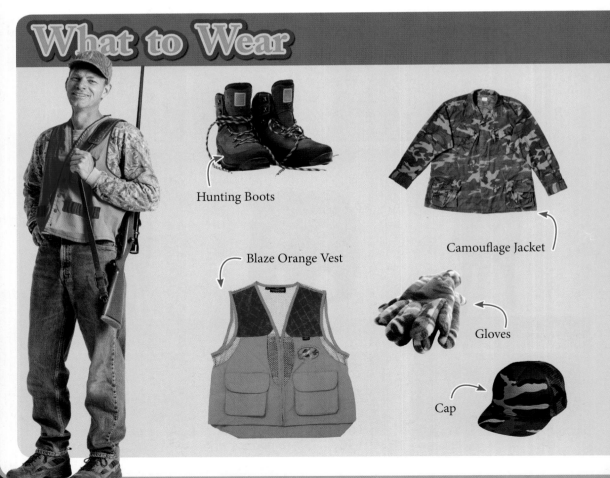

What to Wear

Hunting Boots

Camouflage Jacket

Blaze Orange Vest

Gloves

Cap

Many U.S. states and Canadian provinces require hunters to wear some blaze orange clothing for safety. This color tells other hunters that they are people, not animals. It prevents hunters from shooting other people by accident. Montana, for example, requires hunters to wear at least 400 square inches (2,580 square centimeters) of orange material above their waist. That amount of material is about the size of a safety vest.

Hunters need to take care of their feet. A good pair of hunting boots comes up over the ankle to provide extra support. If the weather is wet, gaiters may be worn. They attach to the top of the boot. Gaiters are made of materials that let sweat escape but help keep water out.

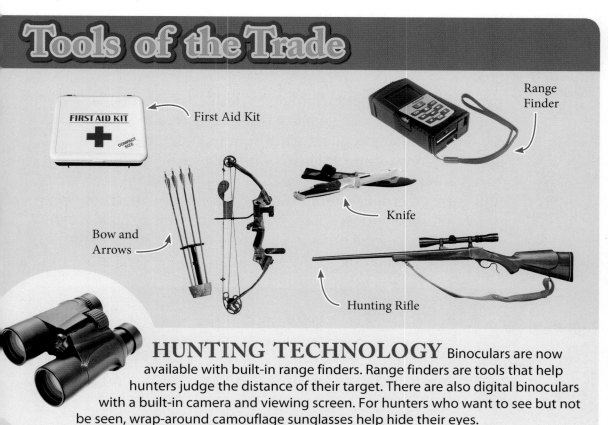

Tools of the Trade

First Aid Kit

Range Finder

Knife

Bow and Arrows

Hunting Rifle

HUNTING TECHNOLOGY Binoculars are now available with built-in range finders. Range finders are tools that help hunters judge the distance of their target. There are also digital binoculars with a built-in camera and viewing screen. For hunters who want to see but not be seen, wrap-around camouflage sunglasses help hide their eyes.

Safety

Big game hunters need to hunt safely. This prevents injury to themselves and to other hunters. Here are some basic safety tips.

Firearm Safety

Knowing the firearm and knowing the target helps everyone stay safe. Treat every firearm as if it were loaded. Always control the gun's muzzle, or firing end. Make sure it never points at anyone. Keep all fingers outside of the **trigger guard** until ready to shoot. Be sure of the target. Be aware of what is in front of and behind the target.

Safety in the Field or Forest

Usually, it is legal to hunt at first light. Hunters often travel through the woods while it is still dark. Wearing a headlamp lights the way and lets other hunters know someone is there. A walking stick helps with balance on rough ground. It is important to be aware of one's surroundings at all times. Carry emergency items, such as a candle and matches. Some hunters carry bear spray. This spray contains pepper. It can stop a bear from pursuing a hunter. It does not harm the bear permanently.

Weather Safety

Check the weather report before heading out. Dress in layers to keep warm. Bring more food than needed for the day. It may start to snow, sleet, or rain. The hunting trip may take longer than expected. Carry extra matches and lighters to start a fire to keep warm. Pack a small first aid kit with an emergency blanket.

Safety in Numbers

Hunting in pairs means one hunter can watch out for the other. If something happens to one hunter, the other can help or go get help. Solo hunters should always let someone else know what their plans are. Someone should know where they are going and when they plan to return.

Be Sure of the Target

Sometimes, hunters think another person is a big-game animal. This mistake leads to one of the most common hunting accidents, which is shooting another person. Wear orange clothing out in the field to be seen more easily. Sometimes, people shoot at targets too close to a farm or road. Other animals or people can get hurt.

Track the FACTS

- Hunting results in fewer incidents involving injuries than many other sports. More injuries occur in cycling, bowling, golf, and tennis than in hunting.

- Most hunting accidents can be avoided. Reasons for accidents include failing to identify the target and careless handling of guns. Guns should be treated as if they can go off at any time.

HUNTER CHECKLIST

1. all necessary paperwork, including a license and hunter education card
2. firearm and ammunition or bow and arrows
3. blaze orange clothing item
4. knives and sharpening stone
5. spotting scope or binoculars
6. Global Positioning System (GPS) device, map, and compass
7. small handsaw
8. 50 feet (15 meters) of thin nylon rope
9. food
10. water
11. cell phone
12. first aid kit
13. flashlight and some extra batteries
14. whistle
15. matches and a lighter
16. rubber gloves for dressing game

Hunting seasons for bow hunters are often longer than they are for hunters who use guns.

Hunting Responsibly

As with any sport, people must follow the rules when hunting. For example, many animals can be hunted only at certain times of the year. In addition, each hunter may be allowed to take only a certain number of animals. Hunters must know the rules regarding their prey. They should encourage other hunters to do the same. National hunting groups encourage hunters to uphold the rules of gun safety. If a hunter is not being careful enough, others should insist on safe behavior.

Licenses and tags are required to hunt big game. A license shows that a hunter has taken a hunting education course. Tags are a way of marking and counting animals. Each captured animal requires a tag. Part of the money that hunters pay for these items goes toward **conservation** research. Conservation helps maintain healthy numbers of animals in nature. Licenses and tags also help government agencies gather information about hunting. This information helps with setting the best dates for the hunting season.

Bows and arrows of different sizes and weights are needed to hunt different animals.

Hunting **ethics** include fair chase. A fair chase means that the animal has a chance to escape. In practice, this means that hunters do not take animals trapped in ice or snow. They do not shoot from cars or boats. Skilled hunters enjoy the challenge of the hunt. It means as much as getting the food or the trophy. Hunting responsibly also means never over-hunting, or taking too many animals. Responsible hunters make sure the animals are taken as quickly as possible.

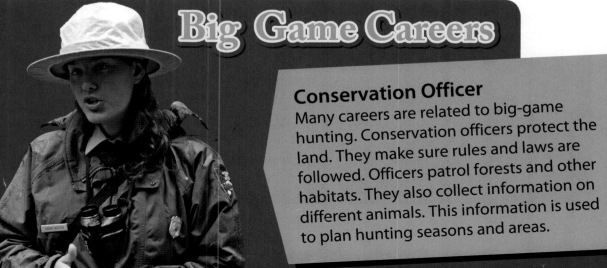

Big Game Careers

Conservation Officer

Many careers are related to big-game hunting. Conservation officers protect the land. They make sure rules and laws are followed. Officers patrol forests and other habitats. They also collect information on different animals. This information is used to plan hunting seasons and areas.

The Rules

To hunt legally, hunters must follow the rules of the area where they are hunting. The rules may vary in different places. Every hunter must complete a hunting safety course before a big-game license is granted. Bow hunting usually requires another kind of permit. Hunters must carry their licenses and permits at all times when looking for game. Otherwise, they can be mistaken for poachers. Those are people who take animals illegally. Poachers either hunt without a license or hunt where it is not allowed, such as on animal **preserves**.

In some areas, the animals are protected from hunters.

Young hunters must be with a licensed adult. In most parts of the United States and in Canada, children under the age of 12 may not hunt. Young hunters, however, can still go with older people on a big-game hunt. There is much to learn and experience in every part of the hunt.

Rules govern hunters' actions. For example, hunters cannot waste the skin of a bear. They must search for any animal that they have wounded. It is the responsibility of all hunters to study and learn the rules for their area.

It helps new hunters to review the rules both before and after a hunt.

Male deer are called bucks because in U.S. frontier days deer hides were worth one dollar.

In 2011, Michigan made it legal for 10-year-olds and 11-year-olds to hunt deer, bears, and elk with a firearm. A licensed adult must be with the young hunters.

At the beginning of the 20th century, white-tailed deer were rare. Today, their numbers have increased. People are allowed to hunt them in national wildlife refuges across the United States.

American Indians in the United States set their own rules for hunting and fishing on their reservations.

After the Hunt

After a successful hunt, hunters must tag their animal. They must also report the animal to a regulation station as soon as possible. These stations tell the government how many animals were taken in a specific area.

Many hunters like to take photos of their catch as well. Afterward, they hang an orange piece of clothing above their head. The bright color alerts other hunters that they are field-dressing the animal they have caught. This is the process of removing the inside parts, which keeps the meat from spoiling.

Connie's Savory Cranberry Pot Roast
(for deer, elk, or moose meat)

Ingredients
1 teaspoon (5 milliliters) oil
4-pound (2-kilogram) boneless pot roast, trimmed of fat
½ teaspoon (2.5 ml) salt
2 cups (0.5 liters) beef broth
½ cup (125 ml) cranberry sauce with whole cranberries
½ cup (125 ml) ketchup
1 envelope of dry onion soup mix
2 cloves of garlic, minced
1 teaspoon (5 ml) Dijon mustard
½ teaspoon (2.5 ml) herbs de Provence
¼ teaspoon (1 ml) black pepper
4 medium potatoes, cut in halves, or new baby potatoes
4 large carrots, cut into quarters

Directions
1. Heat the oil in a large skillet over medium-high heat. Salt the roast and brown it in the skillet. Then, move the meat to a roasting pan.
2. In a bowl, mix the broth, cranberry sauce, ketchup, onion soup mix, garlic, mustard, herbs, and black pepper. Pour the sauce over the roast.
3. Cover and roast at 350° Fahrenheit (175° Celsius) for about 2 hours, basting the meat occasionally.
4. Add the potatoes and carrots. Baste the meat. Cover and roast for another hour. Carve and serve.

Big Game Report

Now it is your turn to go to work. Choose one of the big-game animals listed in the chart on page 7 of this book. Using this book, your school or local library, and the internet, write a report about hunting this animal.

Research tips:

Look for additional books about big-game hunting in your library under the Dewey Decimal number 799.2.

Useful search terms for the internet include "big-game hunting" along with the name of your state or province, "tracking big game," and "moose," "elk," "black bear," or another big-game animal that you have chosen.

Key questions to answer:

1. Where is the animal found?
2. How do you track the animal?
3. When can you hunt the animal?
4. Is there a special tag required for hunting this animal?
5. Why do people hunt this animal?
6. What types of equipment can be used for hunting this animal?

Take Aim Quiz

1 Why do people hunt?

2 What is an atlatl?

3 What tools can help a hunter spot big game from a distance?

4 What is one of the most common accidents that can happen while hunting?

5 Which color clothing is good to wear for safety when hunting?

6 What is a poacher?

7 What is the job of a conservation officer?

8 How old does a person usually have to be to hunt legally?

ANSWERS

1. for food, skins, trophies, and to get outdoors 2. a prehistoric tool used to throw a spear 3. binoculars and spotting scopes 4. mistaking another person for big game and shooting at him or her by accident 5. blaze orange 6. a person who hunts illegally 7. to enforce hunting laws 8. at least age 12

Key Words

conservation: the protection and careful use of forests, rivers, minerals, and other natural resources

ethics: rules of conduct related to a group's behavior

graze: to feed on grasses and other plants

habitat: the place where an animal or plant lives or grows

hibernate: to sleep deeply for an extended period of time in winter

hides: skins of animals, sometimes used to make leather

mammals: warm-blooded animals that have fur or hair and feed their young milk

pemmican: dried meat mixed with fat and berries

preserves: protected, private areas for hunting or fishing

range: the farthest possible distance, such as the distance a gun can shoot

sinews: tough tissues that join muscles to bones or bones to bones

species: groups of individuals with common characteristics

spotting scope: a light telescope that allows one to see animals and objects during the day

trigger guard: a metal or plastic loop around the trigger to help keep the gun from firing

trophy: a record-setting animal or souvenir of a hunt

Index

Log on to www.av2books.com

AV² by Weigl brings you media enhanced books that support active learning. Go to www.av2books.com, and enter the special code found on page 2 of this book. You will gain access to enriched and enhanced content that supplements and complements this book. Content includes video, audio, weblinks, quizzes, a slide show, and activities.

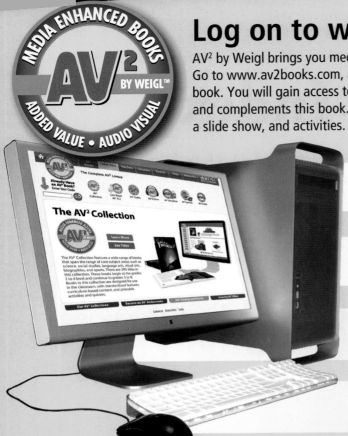

Audio
Listen to sections of the book read aloud.

Video
Watch informative video clips.

Embedded Weblinks
Gain additional information for research.

Try This!
Complete activities and hands-on experiments.

WHAT'S ONLINE?

Try This!	Embedded Weblinks	Video	EXTRA FEATURES
Complete a tracking activity.	Learn more about big game hunting.	Watch a video about big game hunting.	
Identify big game animals.	Find the big game hunting rules for your state.	Watch a video about big game animals.	
Try this matching activity for big game hunting equipment.	Read more about hunting safety.		
Test your knowledge of big game hunting.			

Audio
Listen to sections of the book read aloud.

Key Words
Study vocabulary, and complete a matching word activity.

Slide Show
View images and captio and prepare a presentati

Quizzes
Test your knowledge.

AV² was built to bridge the gap between print and digital. We encourage you to tell us what you like and what you want to see in the future.

Sign up to be an AV² Ambassador at www.av2books.com/ambassador.